Wallace Bruce, John Dawson Ross

From Grant's Tomb to Mt. MacGregor

Patriotic poems and addresses along the Hudson

Wallace Bruce, John Dawson Ross

From Grant's Tomb to Mt. MacGregor
Patriotic poems and addresses along the Hudson

ISBN/EAN: 9783337309572

Printed in Europe, USA, Canada, Australia, Japan

Cover: Foto ©Thomas Meinert / pixelio.de

More available books at **www.hansebooks.com**

FROM

Grant's Tomb to Mt. MacGregor

PATRIOTIC POEMS AND ADDRESSES
ALONG THE HUDSON

BY

WALLACE BRUCE

COLLECTED AND ARRANGED
BY
JOHN D. ROSS, LL.D.,

AUTHOR OF "A CLUSTER OF POETS," "SCOTTISH POETS
IN AMERICA," "SKETCHES ON RANDOM
SUBJECTS," ETC.

BRYANT I
NEW YORK.
1897.

CONTENTS.

	PAGE.
PREFACE.	
AT GRANT'S TOMB,	7
BEND LOW,	9
THE FLAG,	12
At the Grave of General Dix.	
DECORATION DAY,	17
Academy of Music, New York.	
THE STORY OF A PENSION,	20
Yonkers.	
AMERICAN CHARACTERISTICS,	23
Tarrytown.	
THE POWER OF NATIONAL SONG,	28
Haverstraw.	
TRIBUTE TO LINCOLN,	32
Peekskill.	
YORKTOWN,	36
Before an Address at West Point.	
THE LONG DRAMA,	40
Centennial at Newburgh.	

CONTENTS.

	PAGE.
THE FOREST BALLOT, Fishkill.	48
A ROYAL ROUTE, Poughkeepsie.	51
LOVE OF COUNTRY, Poughkeepsie.	56
OUR NATION FOREVER, Rondout.	60
ON GUARD, Tivoli.	62
OUR PRAYER TO-DAY, Saugerties.	66
"VETERANS," Hudson.	69
PARSON ALLEN'S RIDE, Albany.	74
THE COURSE OF FREEDOM, Troy.	78
THE CANDLE PARADE, Saratoga Springs.	80
THE SILENT SOLDIER, Mount MacGregor.	94.

PREFACE.

For many years it has been my custom to make clippings of Addresses and Poems delivered from time to time by our orators and poets, and among these to cherish eloquent selections and graceful incidents of Wallace Bruce.

His recent verses "BEND LOW," warmly received and widely copied throughout the entire country, suggested to me the publication in convenient form of the following popular poems and prose extracts which I have preserved from his various patriotic utterances along the Hudson.

PREFACE.

In response to this idea I was gratified to receive his permission to arrange the same in consecutive order of towns and cities where they have been delivered, thereby attaining pleasant companionship through the beautiful valley he so much loves, and where he has won golden opinions, from the Island of Manhattan to Mount MacGregor at Saratoga.

JOHN D. ROSS.

AT GRANT'S TOMB.

[*From the Christian Advocate.*]

With the departure of the President the multitude of spectators began to melt away, but the long column still continued to move past the tomb, and it was not until the sun was about to set behind the New Jersey hills that the end of the splendid pageant disappeared down the almost deserted drive, and the tomb with its precious dust was enshrouded in the silence of the approaching night. The spirit of the occasion is fittingly characterized in a poem written by Wallace Bruce, and read by him the evening before the dedication at a meeting of the U. S. Grant Post of the Grand Army of the Republic.

Those stars are there in setting blue,
    Because you answered to the call;
We bring no eulogy to you—
    You honor us—you won it all.

BEND LOW.

Dedicated to The Grant Post, Brooklyn, N. Y., whose Guard of Honor stood sentry around the General's Grave.

Bend low beside the Soldier's grave,
    His ashes lift with reverent hand,
Hark to the voice again that gave
    To Liberty supreme command!
Bend low, brave comrades of the past,
    Your garlands strew with moistened eyes,
While angel fingers fondly cast
    Sweet amaranths from waiting skies!

BEND LOW.

Bend low! The world respondeth now
  To echoes from the far away;
Columbia, with uncovered brow,
  A heartfelt offering brings to-day.
Bend low as veteran lips renew
  The glow and throb of burning years;
A people pass in long review
  To pay the homage of their tears.

Bend low! O'er yonder Palisades
  The darkling shadows gently creep;
Bend low while gathering twilight fades
  And starry pickets guard his sleep;
His tomb the Nation's heart for aye
  Reflecting Freedom's fairest beam,
As morning blue and evening gray
  Become the sentries of his dream.

BEND LOW.

Bend low beneath that message fraught
  With prophecy to all the world:—
"Let us have Peace," divinely wrought
  In bannered folds of love unfurled;
His glory as the centuries wide,
  His honor bright as sunlit seas,
His lullaby the Hudson tide,
  His requiem the whispering breeze.

THE FLAG.

AT THE GRAVE OF GEN. DIX.

Decoration Day Tribute at Trinity Cemetery, near Washington Heights.

Dedicated to the John A. Dix Post.

The only factor in the integral of God's sovereignty is the individual; the only factor in the multiple of this great nation is the unit. There were nineteen families in the Mayflower—an indivisible number. There were thirteen stripes and thirteen stars in the old flag, indivisible from its birth. If any man individually wishes to secede, he can come and go at his pleasure. Blackstone defines liberty as the right of locomotion; but no man or body of men can walk off with twenty square feet of the sacred soil of old Virginia or

THE FLAG.

a quarter of a school district in Massachusetts. That question has been decided once and forever.

The serpent of State sovereignty that found its way into the Paradise of our new Republic, and coiled itself Laocoonlike around the limbs of the young nation, has been consigned to a deeper Pandemoniun than dreamed of by Dante or Milton.

The power and supremacy of the flag have been established—the enduring symbol of the nation's authority; and I have great respect for the home-rearing of that little boy who, when asked in Sunday-School, which was the best verse in the Bible, replied, "If any man attempts to haul down the American flag shoot him on the spot." His home-training for American citizenship had not been neglected, and his Apocryphal verse, printed in bold type, would not injure a leaf of any volume of Holy Writ.

You remember how General Dix, who had been Secretary of War only eleven days, sent out that

THE FLAG.

glorious message, the first to thrill the Northern heart. In that sentence, the flag became America! Ten thousand men might have been shot down in the streets of cities in revolt, and some excuse been devised to cover the crime; but when the Flag was assailed, the people of the North came like a great avalanche, increasing as it swept, until two million brave men went to the front in the cause of Liberty.

We stand here to-day, men and women of a great Republic, crowned with the greatest freedom. Do we know how to appreciate its value? Some of you here gathered know what it cost. Count it not in the cold figures of arithmetic or in the value of the individual man in the world's commerce.

By the vacant chairs at so many firesides, by the privations, by the heart agony, by the sleepless nights and long vigils, by the deeds and sufferings of heroic women, by the tears of mother,

THE FLAG.

wife and sister, by the bowed head of the gray-haired man from whom went forth the joy and support of his declining years, by the great army of martyrs, by the brave women who laid down their lives in fever hospitals, and in the presence of that God who listens to the cry of the raven, ay, "caters, providentially for the sparrow," tell me, if you can, the price of yonder symbol?

The offerings that we bring fade away and perish, but the glory you won is immortal. No wonder in the midst of these Providences that the whole land, from the pines of Maine to the forests of the Sierras, on days like these, wakes to the reveille of the morning stars, and brings its offerings to the dead soldiers until night stations her starry pickets above their graves.

Brave boys are they! gone at their country's call! How the old songs come back, and eyes grow dim. Their hands are waiting to clasp yours as of old, and their lips to ask what of the Great

THE FLAG.

Republic for which they died. As one by one you go to join the heroic throng, gathering for the last great muster, take this message, "We have one country, one people, free and united, from gulf to lake, from sea to sea."

DECORATION DAY.

At the Academy of Music, New York.

We deck to-day each soldier's grave,
　We come with offerings pure and white
To bind the brows of those who gave
　Their all to keep our honor bright.

We cannot pay the debt we owe;
　They gave their lives that we might live;
Our warmest words fall far below
　The worship that we fain would give.

O country! fairest of the free;
　Columbia!—name forever blest;
O lost "Atlantis" of the sea!
　Securely anchored in the West;

DECORATION DAY.

Unfold the flag their hands have borne!
   The shreds of many a well-fought field;
The stripes alone are rent and torn,
   The stars are there, our sacred shield.

Those stars are ours because they died,
   The blue is dearer for their sake,
Who sleep on many a green hill-side,
   In ranks that nevermore will break.

For well they wore the color true
   That holds our constellation fair,
And evermore the "Boys in Blue"
   Shall have a day of rest and prayer.

Yes, martyred heroes of the free!
   We kneel beside your mounds and pray
That God our nation's guard may be
   And comrade's hope from day to day.

DECORATION DAY.

O day baptized in blood and tears!
The blood was theirs, the tears are ours;
And children's children through the years
Shall strew their graves with sweetest flowers.

And May-day garlands all in bloom
Will quicken other verse than mine,
And decorate the soldier's tomb
From Southern palm to Northern pine.

THE STORY OF A PENSION.

Decoration Day Address at Yonkers.

A few years ago a woman came to the United States Consulate at Edinburgh. She said while she was a lassie, and working at a mill in Galashiels, there came a soldier one day wearing a blue coat with brass buttons, who had many incidents to narrate of the hardships and heroisms of our civil war. She had read the story of Uncle Tom's Cabin, and knew it by heart; she could recite the poetry of Whittier, which she thought chimed so sweetly with the songs of Robert Burns. He told the story of his life and won her.

They lived happily in Edinburgh, until finally, from sickness contracted in the war he applied to the American Government for a pension. For

THE STORY OF A PENSION.

four years he waited, as the papers came back again and again with new questions, till at last he lay down for two years on a sick bed. His wife and oldest daughter went forth and worked for twenty cents a day, and brought home what they could for the poor, sick sufferer. The doctor at last told him that his end was near, and he said, "Doctor, I have little to give you, except the gun by my bedside." The kind physician said, "I don't want it; it is my business, you know, to heal wounds, not to make them, and I will not charge you anything for my attention." The wife spoke up and said, "We will keep the gun for the poor laddie." The next day, when they turned down the coverlid for the last time, they found he had placed the gun by his side, holding it lovingly against his heart.

So she came and asked for her pension; she had a right to it as the widow of an old soldier. When at last it arrived she said with tears in her

THE STORY OF A PENSION.

eyes, "Oh, if Johnnie could have had it before he died." I asked, "Where is he buried; can we go there on Decoration Day?" And she said, "It is in a Potter's Field; four others have already been buried above him, and it is unmarked." I said to her, "If I live to go to America, I will find sixty men who will give me $100 each; and we will have in the midst of old Edinburgh a plot of ground for the Scottish-American soldiers." I went before the Town Council of Edinburgh and they granted me a site near the Monument of the People dedicated to personal freedom. I had an American sculptor design a statue of "Lincoln Freeing the Slave," to commemorate their deeds, and carved thereon his immortal sentence, dear to every heart: "To preserve the Jewel of Liberty in the Framework of Freedom."

AMERICAN CHARACTERISTICS.

An Address at Tarrytown.

The principal traits of the American are straightforwardness, self-reliance, and readiness to meet emergencies. In a new country like ours people are not given to overmuch ceremony. They have the good old custom of going across lots; they are impatient of fences and old forms; they take the nearest way.

When the authorities of Alexandria forbade the American captain to take down the obelisk, which had been presented to New York by the Khedive of Egypt, he simply wrapped the American flag around it and told his men to proceed. The stripes of that flag were not the sort of red tape that the worthy officials of Alexandria were accustomed to, but no man dared say him nay. That readiness of action revealed his ancestry.

When a certain general, less noted for victories than delays, telegraphed to President Lincoln, "I have captured one hundred cows. What shall I do with them?" the answer consisted of just two words—"milk them." The midnight dispatch of Anthony Wayne to General Washington read: "Stony Point, two o'clock A. M. Dear General, the American flag waves here. Mad Anthony." A dispatch from General Putnam read: "Nathan Palmer was taken as a spy, tried as a spy, and will be hanged as a spy. P. S.—He is hanged." When John Hancock said to the delegates assembled at Philadelphia to discuss the Declaration of Independence, "Gentlemen, we must all hang together." "Yes," said Franklin, "or we will all hang separately."

It is sometimes observed that we have not yet developed a distinctive American literature; but I

AMERICAN CHARACTERISTICS.

believe that no one denies the original flavor of American humor. When a gentleman from Duluth told the English traveler that England was a very good country, but we could put the whole of it into Lake Superior without raising the tide, no one could accuse him of plagiarism. When a group of gentlemen on shipboard were discussing the merits of Vesuvius, and one of the party said, "Bring over your Vesuvius, and we will turn on Niagara Falls and put it out," it was unnecessary to say that the speaker was an American. In a word, there is no cynicism about American humor, but exaggeration, a sense of room and assurance, qualities naturally belonging to a great country, unfenced, untilled, and of boundless resources.

We too often regard the American Revolution as the initial point of our national life; but we must not forget that the great men of the Revolution were the outgrowth of fifty years of self-reliance. They were the descendants of men reared in hard-

AMERICAN CHARACTERISTICS.

ship, of men who carried the Psalms in one hand and the musket in the other. That band of patriots who signed the Declaration of Independence did not spring up by enchantment. That handful of Puritan acorns, shook by the hand of oppression from the topmost bough of the tree of English liberty, deep-rooted on the banks of Runnymede, shipped without bill of lading in the Mayflower, dropped in the rocky soil of New England, neglected and uncared for, became in a century and a half full grown oaks.

If ever in the world's history the words "native mettle" could be applied to any band of men it belongs to the men of 1776. Every field from Bunker Hill to Saratoga and Yorktown revealed the courage and endurance of Saxon blood. Ay, more, in our naval conflicts and in that great struggle, in the memory of many here gathered, we recognize the qualities which inspired the witty toast of the young American fifty years ago in Paris, who, after the rose, the lily, the thistle and the shamrock had been extolled, while his own land had been reduced to an afterthought, responded:

"The lily will fade and its leaves decay,
The rose from its stem dissever,
The thistle and shamrock will pass away,
But the stars shall shine forever."

THE POWER OF NATIONAL SONG.

From an Address at Haverstraw.

The draught of kindness may sparkle with joy but there are tears in the bottom of the cup. Yes, to all of us it speaks of the past; for many who were with us, as it were but yesterday, are now separated by oceans, some by death. Some who went forth with energy and in the strength of manhood to plough furrows of thought through the world, are now sleeping in furrows ploughed deep by cannon-balls—the loved and the lost of our "auld lang syne." But in these lines they all are remembered, although many sleep without a monument along that tract of country where *the fierce fire of battle succeeded in welding a broken union.* Songs which thus find a response in the universal heart of humanity, like those which stir the blood of a nation, have an influence which cannot be measured. Mechanism will give you the force of an engine, the strength of a bridge, or the tension of a cable, but it is impossible to determine the power of an idea which takes hold of the heart and rises to the lips of a nation; and old Fletcher said well, "Let me write the songs of a people, and I care not who make her laws." In the Reformation of Germany, the songs of the Fatherland went hand in hand with the theses of Luther nailed upon the Cathedral doors at Wittenberg. When Knox was driven from his country, the poems of Lyndsay of the Mount were working out his deliverance and the cause of truth. The last Napoleon prohibited years ago the singing of the "Marseillaise Hymn" in the streets of Paris. He knew if that song were raised in the cause of truth, it were mightier than an army with banners. He was literally afraid of that grand stirring chorus, "Marchons, Marchez!" and when I heard it in the dark summer of 1870, as it rose up from the heart of an excited nation bursting its fetters of law, and saw the soldiery kneel as they sang it around the tri-colored flag which had led to so many fields of victory, I thought that if France were only united, rallying around that song, she could withstand the Powers of Europe. Yes, from the invasion of William of Normandy, when Taillifer the minstrel advanced before the army animating them with songs of Charlemagne and Roland, and then rushed among the opposing ranks and perished, until the yesterday of

"Tramp, tramp, tramp, the boys are marching,"

the influence of national songs cannot be measured. The poets who have written them may have died in poverty or in exile. They may have suffered martyrdom at the stake or at the bar of public opinion; but their lines live, the

THE POWER OF NATIONAL SONG.

monument of their exile and the crown of their martyrdom. You may burn the writer, but the fire only melts the links of tyranny. A true poet cannot be a slave. He feels deeply, and liberty is his inspiration. He knows there is an honor more sacred than law, a natural veneration more effective than enacted statutes. National honor is stronger than political bulwarks. This is the boundary of a Divine Providence. Political bulwarks are often the mere mud-dykes of a generation.

TRIBUTE TO LINCOLN.

Address at Peekskill.

We have no primogeniture of greatness, but what we might term a natural succession or heredity of wit. Not only that wit which says the right thing at the right time, but also does the right thing at the right moment. I take it that Abraham Lincoln is the natural descendant of Benjamin Franklin. They both were emphatically the architects of their own fortunes. They sprang from the common mass, inheriting and retaining the qualities of the people—hospitality, fidelity, sympathy and common sense. The sayings of each are national proverbs. "It is'nt safe to swap horses while crossing the stream" was the closing sentence of Lincoln's address accepting renomination, and that one sentence was worth a hundred thousand campaign speeches.

TRIBUTE TO LINCOLN.

On his way to assist at the dedication of the National Cemetery and Monument at Gettysburg he unfolded a newspaper, and, pointing to five long closely printed columns, said to a friend: "Here is the speech of Edward Everett, which he is to deliver to-day, already in type." Then, taking from his vest-pocket a torn yellow official envelope, written with pencil, and marked with erasures, he said: "Here is mine." The speech of the great Massachusett's orator has become the property of mouldy scrap-books, but the pencilled sentences on the torn yellow envelope will live in the American heart as long as the stars shine in the sky. "It is not what we say here, but what they did here." His detractors called him rude and uncouth, and the London newspapers, forsooth, said that we had elected a mountebank for President.

In the age of Pericles two statues were made by rival sculptors. The one that received the approval of the people was to be placed on high in their temple. The statues were unveiled; one received the plaudits, the other the derision of the assembly. "Lift it to its place," said the unsuccessful sculptor. The approved statue was lifted; the lines of beauty were all gone. "Lift mine." As the great statue reached the lofty pedestal a shout burst from the excited throng. So seemed the rugged qualities of that noble man lifted to the proudest pinnacle of a nation's love.

When I think of the detractors of men like Lincoln I am somehow reminded of Mark Twain's description of the Sphynx in his "Innocence Abroad;" that grand image of retrospection and memory, gazing out over the ocean of time, a great statue, sixty feet high, one hundred and twenty-five feet long, carved out of a solid block of stone, harder than iron. He heard, you remember, the clink of a hammer, and there, way up on the cheek of the Sphynx, saw something resembling a wart. "It seems," he said, "that one of our well-meaning reptiles, a relic hunter, had crawled up there, and was trying to break off a specimen; but the great image, unconscious of the small insect that was fretting the granite in vain, was contemplating the ages as calmly as ever." Lincoln's detractors and critics are all gone. The lines in Punch over the plain coffin at Springfield confessed at last that he had lived to shame them from their sneer:

" Our shallow judgments we have learned to rue,
   Noting how to occasion's height he rose :
How his quaint wit made home truth seem more true,
   How iron-like his temper grew by blows."

Ay, a tower has been erected to his memory in London, a monument in Edinburgh. The streets of Italian cities have been named in his honor; his portrait hangs in the humble cottages of the Swiss mountaineer, and his name is affectionately remembered in the hearts of the oppressed all over the world.

YORKTOWN.

Prefacing a Lecture at West Point.

To the Memory of John Bruce, Sergeant at Lexington.

We stand to-day on Yorktown field,
   Where Britain laid her banner down,
Where tyranny to freedom kneeled,
   And dropped the jewels from her crown.

We gather here from every land,
   With offerings brought from near and far,
Like men of old—the Eastern band—
   Led onward by the Western star.

We meet around an humble shrine,
   We mark the spot with graven stone,
A trophy to that Right Divine
   Whereby to manhood we have grown.

YORKTOWN.

Our hundred years of youth have passed,
    With deeds that prove the Nation brave,
And strife and jealousy at last
    Lie buried in one common grave.

One flag floats over all the land,
    One sentiment thrills every heart;
No foreign foe, no factious band,
    The land we love shall ever part.

The past is sure, the future waits;
    The years with enterprise are rife;
With hope the century celebrates
    The birthday of a nation's life.

We measure time by glorious deeds;
    All history is simply this:
It skips the years; it merely reads
    From Marathon to Salamis.

YORKTOWN.

We gather courage from the past,
   And from heroic pages learn:
Triumphant freedom finds at last
   A Runnymede or Bannockburn.

Ay, every struggle to be free
   'Gainst courtly craft and regal might,
Preserves the line of liberty,
   And keeps her armor clean and bright.

The sceptre and the diadem
   In ev'ry land shall lose their power,
Freedom's the only flawless gem,
   And equal rights the people's dower.

The diamond in the monarch's crown
   Is crystallized from peasants' tears;
The purple of his royal gown
   Betokens blood of bitter years.

YORKTOWN.

The scaffold stairs which Sidney trod
   Led from the dungeon to the sky;
The tyrant sways a feeble rod
   When patriots dare to do and die.

Grander the manger than the throne;
   "Free hearts and hands," the poet sings;
Freedom and faith and these alone,
   "The grace of God," but not of kings.

THE LONG DRAMA.

Read at the Centennial of the Disbanding of the American Army, Newburgh, N. Y.

With banners bright, with roll of drums,
    With pride and pomp and civic state,
A nation, born of courage, comes
    The closing act to celebrate.

We've traced the drama page by page
    From Lexington to Yorktown field;
The curtain drops upon the stage,
    The century's book to-day is sealed.

A cycle grand—with wonders fraught
    That triumph over time and space—
In woven steel its dreams are wrought,
    The nations whisper face to face.

THE LONG DRAMA.

But in the proud and onward march
    We halt an hour for dress parade,
Remembering that fair freedom's arch
    Springs from the base our fathers laid.

With cheeks aglow with patriot fire
    They pass in long review again;
We grasp the hand of noble sire
    Who made two words of " Noblemen."

In silence now the tattered band—
    Heroes in homespun worn and gray—
Around the old Headquarters stand,
    As in that dark, uncertain day.

That low-roofed dwelling shelters still
    The phantom tenants of the past;
Each garret beam, each oaken sill,
    Treasures and holds their memories fast.

THE LONG DRAMA.

Ay, humble walls! the manger-birth
   To emphasize this truth was given:
The noblest deeds are nearest earth,
   The lowliest roofs are nearest heaven.

We hear the anthem once again—
   "No king but God!"—to guide our way,
Like that of old—"Good-will to men"—
   Unto the shrine where freedom lay.

One window looking toward the east;
   Seven doors wide-open every side;
That room revered proclaims at least
   An invitation free and wide.

Wayne, Putnam, Knox, and Heath are there;
   Steuben, proud Prussia's honored son;
Brave Lafayette from France the fair,
   And, chief of all, our Washington.

THE LONG DRAMA.

Serene and calm in peril's hour,
    An honest man without pretence,
He stands supreme to teach the power
    And brilliancy of common-sense.

Alike disdaining fraud and art,
    He blended love with stern command;
He bore his country in his heart,
    He held his army by the hand.

Hush! carping critic, read aright
    The record of his fair renown:
A leader by diviner right
    Than he who wore the British crown.

With silvered locks and eyes grown dim,
    As victory's sun proclaimed the morn,
He pushed aside the diadem
    With stern rebuke and patriot scorn.

THE LONG DRAMA.

He quells the half-paid mutineers,
   And binds them closer to the cause;
His presence turns their wrath to tears,
   Their muttered threats to loud applause.

The great republic had its birth
   That hour beneath the army's wing,
Whose leader taught by native worth
   The man is grander than the king.

The stars on that bright azure field,
   Which proudly wave o'er land and sea,
Were fitly taken from his shield
   To be our common heraldry.

We need no trappings worn and old,
   No courtly lineage to invoke,
No tinselled plate, but solid gold,
   No thin veneer, but heart of oak.

THE LONG DRAMA.

No aping after foreign ways
   Becomes a son of noble sire;
Columbia wins the sweetest praise
   When clad in simple, plain attire.

In science, poesy, and art,
   We ask the best the world can give;
We feel the throb of Britain's heart,
   And will while Burns and Shakespeare live.

But, oh! the nation is too great
   To borrow emptiness and pride:
The queenly Hudson wears in state
   Her robes with native pigments dyed.

October lifts with colors bright
   Its mountain canvas to the sky;
The crimson trees, aglow with light,
   Unto our banners wave reply.

THE LONG DRAMA.

Like Horeb's bush the leaves repeat
    From lips of flame with glory crowned:
"Put off thy shoes from off thy feet,
    The place they trod is holy ground."

O fairest stream beneath the sun!
    Thy Highland portal was the key
Which force and treason wellnigh won,
    Like that of famed Thermopylæ.

That ridge along our eastern coast,
    From Carolina to the Sound,
Opposed its front to Britain's host,
    And heroes at each pass were found—

A vast primeval palisade,
    With bastions bold and wooded crest,
A bulwark strong by nature made
    To guard the valley of the West.

THE LONG DRAMA.

Along its heights the beacons gleamed;
    It formed the nation's battle-line,
Firm as the rocks and cliffs where dreamed
    The soldier-seers of Palestine.

These hills shall keep their memory sure,
    The blocks we rear shall fall away,
The mountain fastnesses endure,
    And speak their glorious deeds for aye.

And oh! while morning's golden urn
    Pours amber light o'er purple brim,
And rosy peaks like rubies burn
    Around the emerald valley's rim,

So long preserve our hearthstone warm!
    Our reverence, O God, increase!
And let the glad centennials form
    One long millennial of peace.

THE FOREST BALLOT.

Before an Address at Fishkill.

When the trees their ballots cast,
    And the forests all are polled,
Which will win the suffrage vast—
    Crimson leaves or leaves of gold?

In the radiant autumn days,
    Silently on hill and wold,
Through the amber-tinted haze,
    Fall the leaves of red and gold—

Leaves that keep the cruel stain
    Of the blood of brothers dead,
Symbols of a nation's pain:
    Count them sadly—leaves of red;

THE FOREST BALLOT.

Leaves that hold the mellow light
   Of the stars on banner-fold,
Symbols of enduring right:
   Count them gladly—leaves of gold;

Emblems those of dire defeat,
   Emblems these of courage bold;
Which will triumph, which is meet—
   Crimson leaves or leaves of gold?

By the record of the past,
   By that story proudly told,
By fair freedom won at last,
   Crimson yields to leaves of gold.

By the faith that conquers doubt,
   Right will triumph as of old.
See! The red is fading out,
   Clearer glow the tints of gold.

THE FOREST BALLOT.

So, when all the leaves are cast,
    And the forest vote is polled,
With a suffrage wide and vast
    Victory crowns the leaves of gold.

A ROYAL ROUTE.

FROM GETTYSBURG TO ATLANTA—FROM ATLANTA TO THE SEA.

Reunion of the One Hundred and Fiftieth New York Regiment at Poughkeepsie.

Dedicated to its first Colonel, Gen. John H. Ketcham.

Gay-bannered streets a greeting speak,
    And standards bright with storied name;
While moistened eye and burning cheek
    Unite proud welcome to proclaim.

But waving plumes are symbols cold
    To voice what Dutchess here would say—
And speech is silver, silence gold,
    When memories o'er our heartstrings play.

A ROYAL ROUTE.

The same rich glory floods the land,
   October flings her colors out,
As when your noble, loyal band
   Went forth upon its royal route;

To bear yon flag, which loved ones gave,
   Through forest, plain, and mountains vast;
Our father's heritage to save,
   To keep fair freedom's title fast—

At Gettysburg, where fate and fame
   Three days the wreath of victory tossed
From hill to hill through battery-flame,
   From line to line where courage crossed—

In Tennessee, where Lookout Height
   With thunder-tone revealed the law,
A cloud-wreathed Sinai, clad with might—
   Resaca, Dallas, Kenesaw—

A ROYAL ROUTE.

And nameless fields where valor led,
  As Hooker blazed his southward way,
Till Allatoona heard the tread
  Of Sherman's troops that came to stay.

I've walked those rugged mountain ways
  Where echoes sleep 'mid tranquil joys;
Have waked the hills with notes of praise,
  And touched my hat to "Ketcham's Boys."

Have marked the fields whereon they stood,
  With pride for Dutchess, tried and true,
And deemed each spot a holy rood,
  Made sacred by the Boys in Blue.

O grand old Twentieth Army Corps!
  Our hearts go out to thee and thine—
Seven thousand reached Atlanta's door
  Of seventeen thousand men in line.

A ROYAL ROUTE.

Dark, cruel days! Ten thousand lost!
    Engulfed in war's encrimsoned tide;
A fearful price! but worth the cost—
    The land is free for which they died.

Then who would grudge to men like these
    The pensioned pittance of a crust?
Strike down yon flag that flaunts the breeze,
    And all your wealth is glittering dust.

A land with honor gone is naught,
    The people want no huckstering cry;
Too rich the realm for which they fought
    To let her brave defenders die.

The wires are cut. The army swings
    Through seas of pine from moorings free;
With Slocum now the Twentieth sings
    The March through Georgia to the Sea.

A ROYAL ROUTE.

And so the deep, proud chorus swells
  From north to south through all the land—
A symphony of golden bells
  Swung by the Great Director's hand;

Till every state from east to west
  Takes up Columbia's glorious chant—
Faith, freedom, hope, and truth abreast—
  With grand *crescendo* under Grant.

LOVE OF COUNTRY.

DECORATION DAY SERVICE.

At Hamilton Post Poughkeepsie.

The safeguard of a government is not in its armories. It is rather in the love of country. We have a right to love our city and its institutions; a right to be proud of our colleges and schools; a right to speak of the taste and culture of this, the fair city of the Empire State.

You, gentlemen, in taking the name of your Post did not have to go outside of this city to find one of the noblest, one of the worthiest names in our American History—the name of Hamilton. It was fitting, Veterans of Poughkeepsie, ay, for many reasons, that you should have

LOVE OF COUNTRY.

selected this name. It not only takes us back to the day when the Constitution of the United States was ratified in the city of Poughkeepsie by the argument and zeal of Alexander Hamilton, but it binds together three generations of heroes. You take your name from the heroic grandson, who rests to-day beneath the roses and the tears of a nation's gratitude; but the middle link of that illustrious chain, at once *son* and *sire*, still remains to us—our respected citizen, Hon. Philip Hamilton, who was with us in our procession, and stood uncovered during these impressive exercises. It is indeed our privilege to love Poughkeepsie, and refer with pride to her illustrious names.

We have a right to revere the County of Dutchess; to love the great State of New York, appropriately titled the Empire State, with its well deserved motto "Excelsior;" we have a right to be proud of a commonwealth which contains within its borders one-tenth of the population of this great land. Look at its glorious *framework* and *picture:*

The Hudson, not only punctuated with beauty, but also with historic names and dramatic incidents from the sea to the wilderness. Behold Stony Point and West Point and Newburgh; Stillwater, Saratoga and Bemis Heights; Lake George, with its history and its scenery, and Lake Champlain, with its blended record of 1776 and of 1812. We have on the north the Thousand Islands and the Rapids of the St. Lawrence, and Lake Ontario, and Lake Erie, whose waters seem to speak the power and grandeur of the "Great West," in the falls of Niagara; to the south we find the valley of the Wyoming and the beautiful Delaware Water Gap. What a grand framework it is! Well, now for the picture. We see the Catskills and the Adirondacks, and Otsego Lake, where Cooper lived, and the placid valley

LOVE OF COUNTRY.

"where the Mohawk gently glides;" we see Watkins Glen, the beautiful cascades around the modern Ithaca, the falls of the Genesee, and the garden land about Rochester. Ay, this is a grand State. We have a right to love it with its majestic framework and superb picture. But how idle to stop here, when we think of the grand extent of this glorious country united forever in the bonds of peace. I recall the speech of a great orator, Dr. Chapin, at Hudson, N. Y., during the days of the Civil War. He referred to the silver lakes of the north, the rockbound Atlantic, the golden sands of the Pacific and the Gulf of Mexico. Then stepping forward from the lecture desk, he exclaimed: "This grand and glorious wedding ring of our Fathers, with the tomb of Washington for a signet."

OUR NATION FOREVER.

Preluding an Address at Rondout.

Ring out to the stars the glad chorus!
    Let bells in sweet melody chime;
Ring out to the sky bending o'er us
    The chant of a nation sublime:
One land with a history glorious!
One God and one faith all victorious.

The songs of the camp-fires are blended,
    The North and the South are no more;
The conflict forever is ended,
    From the lakes to the palm-girded shore.

One people united forever
    In hope greets the promising years;
No discord again can dissever
    A Union cemented by tears.

OUR NATION FOREVER.

The past will retain but one story—
 A record of courage and love;
The future shall cherish one glory,
 While the stars shine responsive above.

With emotions of pride and of sorrow,
 Bring roses and lilies to-day;
In the dawn of the nation's to-morrow
 We garland the Blue and the Gray.
One land with a history glorious!
One God and one faith all victorious!

ON GUARD.

THE ONE HUNDRED AND FIFTIETH NEW YORK REGIMENT AT GETTYSBURG.

Recited at a Sabbath Decoration Day Address at Tivoli.

We can not consecrate this field,
   Or hallow ground where heroes stood;
Thus spoke the man whose words have sealed
   Our lips in Freedom's Holy Rood.

We can not dedicate. Too well
   Our Lincoln knew the Temple's cost,
He heard the nation's anthem swell:
   Your deeds survive, our words are lost.

ON GUARD.

The brave men living and the dead,
   Who wrought the epic of the free,
Have consecrated here, he said,
   The land, the world, to liberty.

And now amid the whirling years
   That punctuate the swift decades,
You come with blended joy and tears,
   In peace beneath the gathering shades,

To contemplate from hill to hill
   The line you held those bitter days,
Again to feel your pulses thrill,
   Once more to take your meed of praise;

With noble monument to mark
   The spot where Dutchess, tried and true,
Stood by the faith when skies were dark,
   And stars were blotted from the blue;

ON GUARD.

A picket outpost here for aye
  With watchword of the Hudson born,
To note the moonlight shadows play,
  To greet with joy the early morn;

A silent sentinel to keep
  Its post along the quiet line;
A Bannockburn, where brothers sleep—
  A Waterloo, where roses twine.

Ay, Gettysburg, thy name at last
  Proclaims the triumph of the race;
'Tis here the future greets the past,
  And faith asserts her crowning grace.

No other battle-field like thine,
  Where love joins hands across the way,
One flag, one land, a sacred shrine
  Alike unto the Blue and Gray.

ON GUARD.

Then rear the graven stone with pride
   Along the line where freedom's van
Proclaims to generations wide
   The final victory of man:

That love and law will reign supreme
   Where'er the starry banner waves,
When stones that now in sunlight gleam
   Crumble to dust above their graves.

OUR PRAYER TO-DAY.

Memorial Address at Saugerties.

Our prayer to-day is that these scenes may not be re-enacted. Some years ago on one of our River steamboats an old gentleman remarked, as we were passing under Kosciusko's monument, "It has been fifty years since I have seen the Hudson River. In the year 1839 I graduated at West Point." He said, "I live in Tennessee, and I felt it my duty to fight on the side of the South. One day, near New Orleans, I was posted behind some cotton bales as a breastwork, firing at a Union ship." He told me that his son had graduated from the Naval Academy, and that the son fought under the stars and stripes. He said, "Many times that day I touched the cannon

OUR PRAYER TO-DAY.

which sent havoc into that vessel, and finally, at night-fall, after the battle was over, I received a message that my son was lying dead upon its deck;" and he added: "I always thought, and I feel to-day, that it was my own hand that sent my son into eternity." Then, with tears flowing down his cheeks, he exclaimed: "My friend, never fire at the stars and stripes, and never forget your country."

I see some here who know pages of this bitter history by heart; some to whom this day is not an idle form; some who dropped tears with the flowers that they placed upon their comrades' graves; some who in the long nights have outwatched the stars; some who have heard the roll-call of names which knew no response save the sobs of some distant fire-side. I see men here who were in the fire of battle and looked death in the face, with calm heroism, where leaden dice seemed hurled by the hand of fate—

OUR PRAYER TO-DAY.

men such as Cromwell spoke of—men who could think with their bayonets, and more than that, men who could pray, and there are no words that can add any glory or any tribute to what they have done.

I stood but yesterday before another assemblage like this. I saw similar flags to these which are about me now—flags all faded and fretted out, with the names of Gettysburg and Antietam upon them, and the long roll of battlefields that we know by heart; and I saw that the stripes had all been worn away and only the stars were left, and I felt that the flags symbolized the long struggle and the grand result.

"VETERANS."

*Re-union of the One Hundred and Twenty-eighth
Regiment New York State Volunteers
at Hudson.*

Dedicated to the memory of Col. Cowles.

One word on our lips, and but one to-day;
  One word in our hearts as we gather here,
Enshrined in our annals to live for aye,
  To freedom and freemen forever dear.

But how shall we utter with reverence meet
  That word where emotions are more than speech,
When martyred heroes comrades greet,
  And voices from Heaven's high ramparts reach!

"VETERANS."

Go, speak it in whispers where daisies free
   On a million mounds with dews are wet!
Herald with trumpet from sea to sea
   The word that a nation will not forget!

Attune it to music that thrills the soul
   With old-time fervor remembered yet!
The smoke-stained banner again unroll!
   The stars in their courses will not forget.

Engrave it in marble of purest white;
   In granite columns its letters set;
Ay, trace it with pencils of living light
   The blue-domed heavens will not forget.

These walls proclaim it in glory; behold!
   A loyal welcome to noble sons;
Through floral lips to brothers bold
   One word, and that word—"Veterans."

"*VETERANS.*"

We bow before it; our all is there—
  Our flag, our freedom, our land and pride,
Our country's fame and promise fair—
  The world's great future with outlook wide.

For that banner is more than painted gauze;
  It voices the hopes of a thousand years—
A registered charter of sacred laws,
  Full covenant purchased by blood and tears.

You know its value, survivors few—
  Three hundred now of a thousand then,
Who marched from our camp in proud review;
  The star-dotted roll-call read again.

Absent! Sleeping at Camp Parapet,
  On Chalmette field and at Quarantine,
With salt-driven spray the roster is wet,
  At Port Hudson's dismal and wild ravine—

"VETERANS."

Where brave men spoke with bated breath,
    As brothers fell in that murderous blast;
While fate shook leaden dice with death,
    And cheeks grew pale as the die was cast.

A black steed dashes across the plain,
    With foam-flecked bridle streaming free,
A gallant and noble soldier slain,
    Your leader through centuries yet to be.

Who, fighting, "fell with face to the foe,"
    And sent it a message to sorrowing souls—
Imperial sentence! with Spartan glow,
    On record immortal—our brave Colonel Cowles.

Ah, well we recall the silent street,
    When that horse was led to the hero's grave,
With army-cloak on saddle-seat,
    And the flag that he gave his life to save.

"VETERANS."

And well we remember your record, boys,
   In the years that followed when days were dark,
As through the Red Sea with steady poise
   Our citizen soldiers bore Liberty's ark.

And children's children your deeds will relate,
   And cherish your memories ever dear,
The gallant One Hundred and Twenty-eight,
   Which in days of peril answered—" Here!"

Ay, long as the stately Hudson flows,
   Or the Catskills sentinel-duty keep,
While Roeleffe Jansen singing goes,
   And binds our counties in crystal sweep;

Till the fame of our fathers has faded away,
   Till the stars of the old dear banner set,
Till the gold of the sunlight is sprinkled with gray—
   Columbia and Dutchess will not forget.

PARSON ALLEN'S RIDE.

Before address in the old Tweddle Hall, Albany.

THE " Catamount Tavern " is lively to-night,
   The boys of Vermont and New Hampshire are here,
All drawn up in line in the lingering light,
   To greet Parson Allen with shout and with cheer.

Over mountain and valley, from Pittsfield Green,
   Through the driving rain of that August day,
The "Flock" marched on with martial mien,
   And the Parson rode in his "one-horse shay."

" Three cheers for old Berkshire!" the General said,
   As the boys of New England drew up face to face.
" Baum bids us a breakfast to-morrow to spread,
   And the Parson is here to say us the ' grace.' "

PARSON ALLEN'S RIDE.

"The lads who are with me have come here to fight,
    And we know of no grace," was the Parson's reply,
"Save the name of Jehovah, our country and right,
    Which your own Ethan Allen pronounced at
        Fort Ti."

"To-morrow," said Stark, "there'll be fighting to do,
    If you think you can wait for the morning light;
And, Parson, I'll conquer the British with you,
    Or Molly Stark sleeps a widow at night."

What the Parson dreamed in that Bennington camp
    Neither Yankee nor Prophet would dare to guess;
A vision, perhaps, of the King David stamp,
    With a mixture of Cromwell and good Queen Bess.

But we know the result of that glorious day,
    And the victory won ere the night came down;
How Warner charged in the bitter fray
    With Rossiter, Hobart, and old John Brown!

PARSON ALLEN'S RIDE.

And how, in a lull of the three-hours' fight,
    The Parson harangued the Tory line
As he stood on a stump, with his musket bright,
    And sprinkled his texts with the powder fine:

"The sword of the Lord is our battle cry,
    A refuge sure in the hour of need,"
And freedom and faith can never die
    Is article first of the Puritan creed.

"Perhaps the 'occasion' was rather rash,"
    He remarked to his comrades after the rout;
"For behind a bush I saw a flash,
    But I fired that way and put it out."

And many the sayings, eccentric and queer,
    Repeated and sung through the whole country-side,
And quoted in Berkshire for many a year,
    Of the Pittsfield march and the Parson's ride.

PARSON ALLEN'S RIDE.

All honor to Stark and his resolute men,
 To the Green Mountain Boys all honor and praise,
While with shout and with cheer we welcome again
 The Parson who rode in his one-horse chaise.

THE COURSE OF FREEDOM.

*Peroration of Address on "The Hudson,"
Delivered at Troy.*

How the sublime and beautiful in the material world are interwoven with the political and moral development of a people! We can not live in the midst of majestic scenery without feeling its inspiration in our hearts, inciting us to something nobler and better.

It is impossible to be slaves where all nature speaks of liberty. In tracing the progress of freedom from the time when the Reformation electrified Europe, we see her first footsteps, like the approach of morning, upon the mountains and along the banks of rivers!

We see her light illumine the clear streams of Switzerland, we hear her voice from mountain-walled Geneva; till almost exiled from Europe, she takes up the words of Knox, "Give me Scotland or I die;" and in the deep fastnesses of her hills, and in the deeper hearts of a people who drank in liberty with the very air they breathed, awaited patiently the hour of proclaiming to the world the right of private judgment, both in religion and in politics; ever teaching that noble sentiment of loyalty to conviction, which led Charles the First through the windows of Whitehall upon the scaffold, and banished the House of Stuart from the Throne of England.

She crosses the ocean and lays here the foundation of a Republic, where civil and religious government becomes civil and religious liberty, and the Divine Right of Kings becomes the Divine Rights of Men. And here along our fair rivers a nobler Freedom shall ever flourish, and along this the fairest stream will gather Poetry from its Legends, Hope from its History, and a Consciousness of God from its Beauty.

THE CANDLE PARADE.

Eighteenth Reunion of the Society of the Army of the Potomac at Saratoga Springs.

[After the Army of the Potomac had returned from the capture of Richmond to Alexandria, a single company, each man with a lighted candle in his gun, marched one night throughout the camps in sportive procession. Regiments and brigades caught the spirit, until fifty thousand candles were immediately converted into weird-like battalions wheeling and dancing along the hillsides in every direction.]

Once again Potomac's army answers to the muster-roll;
Once again the old-time music thrills the soldier's heart and soul.
Rank on rank, with cheer and gladness, rally at the bugle-call
On the field of Saratoga, underneath its mountain-wall,

THE CANDLE PARADE.

Where MacGregor's evening shadows fall upon the
  crystal tide,
At the gate-way of the cottage where the nation's
  hero died;
Where the streams in gentle music still our father's
  requiem chant,
And the pine, the oak, the maple, and the laurel
  echo—Grant.

Name revered, that clasps great rivers evermore in
  loving thrall:
Queenly Hudson, fair Potomac, Mississippi—king
  of all;
Rivers three, that bind one nation from the Gulf
  to Northern lakes,
From the Rockies to Virginia, where the loud
  Atlantic breaks;
Arms entwined and interlocking, holding in their
  wide embrace

THE CANDLE PARADE.

Sweeping hills and lordly mountains of the Appalachian race;
Fertile fields and rolling prairies with their wealth of floral bloom,
Plucked and borne by loving fingers to the loyal Logan's tomb.

Fruit of gold in silver pictures—waving fields by rivers framed;
States discordant reunited, love and land and flag reclaimed:
Fruit of gold—a century's harvest, in war's reaping rudely shorn—
Garnered heroes, named and nameless, swift on fiery chariots borne.
Rest in peace by stately rivers, martyred soldiers of the free!
Rest, brave captain, at our threshold, where the Hudson meets the sea!

THE CANDLE PARADE.

While Mount Vernon's sacred portal sentinels Potomac's waves,
Mississippi sends her greetings to the streams that guard their graves.

Fair Potomac! dear Potomac! at thy name what memories throng!
Deeds of heroism blazoned in a nation's art and song.
Onward sweeps the steady column to the sound of fife and drum;
Solid phalanx, proud battalion; see the sun-browned veterans come.
Forward, to the touch of elbow, as of old in long review:
Missing comrades take their places in the ranks that wear the blue.
"On to Richmond!" "On to Richmond!" swells the old familiar cry.

THE CANDLE PARADE.

"On this line"—you know the context—comes
    the soldier's brief reply.

Southward now, with ranks concentring, reads the
    order of the day,
Wilderness and Spottsylvania marking halts along
    the way,
Where the trees are mowed with bullets—brothers
    battling hand to hand—
Blue and Gray, with kindred courage worthy of
    one fatherland;
Both alike in silent trenches guarding now the
    peaceful scene,
Waiting till the morn's reveille wakes the camps
    of waving green.
Southward still across North Anna, thirty miles
    from Rapidan;
Southward, by the left flank marching, gallant
    Hancock in the van.

THE CANDLE PARADE.

How each message, fraught with glory, taught a listening land the names
Of the Old Dominion rivers, from Potomac to the James!
How you kept the "Dailies" busy with their topographic maps—
One eye on the Shenandoah, one on Sherman's shoulder-straps!
Sheridan in rapid orbit, like a genuine son of Mars,
Sherman on the outer circle, Saturn-like among the stars;
Here and there a warlike comet—dauntless Custer, dashing "Kil;"
But they had to "get up Early" to compete with "Little Phil."

Who can paint that panorama, clear and perfect in detail?

THE CANDLE PARADE.

Who can trace the telling bullets in that storm of leaden hail?
Who can twine a fitting garland for each dear heroic name,
Or untwist the strands of glory in the cable of our fame?
This sufficeth and abideth—every thread is firm and true;
Homespun texture, double woven, colors fast—red, white, and blue;
Knotted well at Appomattox, tied to keep the threads in place,
Never more to be unravelled in the nation's onward race.

Homeward now with flaunting banners, every heart with triumph thrills;
Homeward to the old-time quarters on the Alexandria hills.

THE CANDLE PARADE.

Once again a thousand camp-fires on the wide
  horizon glow;
Once again the canvas city spreads its tents of
  drifted snow;
All the long, fierce conflict over, day of Jubilee
  is here;
No more longing, no more waiting—give us,
  boys, a song of cheer.
Hail the bright-illumined city, with its crowning
  dome of white!
Hail Columbia! hail Potomac! All the land is
  free to-night!

What is that along the hill-side? See a hundred
  twinkling points
Starting up and gliding slowly, serpent-like with
  glittering joints.
Mark the sweeping curves of beauty as in waving
  lines it breaks,

THE CANDLE PARADE.

Holding all the wide encampment in its folds of fiery flakes—
Solid squares and ranks of twinkle putting phantasy to shame;
Phosphorous billows in the darkness gemmed with drifting dots of flame;
Ghostly folds of sable serge-cloth trimmed with glittering golden braid;
Spirit-lights of weird battalions dancing all in masquerade.

You remember well the sombre silence of that vision vast;
As a background for the pageant, all the sky was overcast.
Then upon the stillness breaking came the old familiar airs,
Choral links of home and camp-fire treasured in a nation's prayers—

THE CANDLE PARADE.

"Home, Sweet Home" and "John Brown's Body,"
  "Dixie-Land" and "Old Camp-ground,"
Swinging symphonies commingled in one bright
  bouquet of sound.
Then from out the ruddy petals "Forward!"
  came the order shrill,
And the visioned scene was mortal—'twas the
  famous candle-drill.

No one knew just how it started, how that
  strange parade began,
Emblem of the nation's genius and the individual
  man;
Waiting not lieutenant's order, epaulette or crim-
  son sash,
Blending in the ready impulse Saxon grit and
  Gaelic dash.
Here, perhaps, a lighted candle in a musket,
  just for play,

THE CANDLE PARADE.

Then a score, platoon, battalion—all the scene is under way,
And the chorus, proudly swelling, stirs the heart of every corps,
"We are coming, Father Abram, fifty thousand candles more."

We are coming, we are coming, as of old the army came—
"Wide Awakes" and "Little Giants," in one lava stream of flame,
Knowing but one common duty when the banner was defied,
Stirred in every nerve and fibre when the gallant Ellsworth died.
Steadfast Lincoln, Douglas greets you with his followers tried and true:
"Keep for aye the nation's honor, all the stars within the blue."

THE CANDLE PARADE.

Noble hero! generous rival! both, alas, too soon to fall.
Lincoln! still the Douglas greets you, "Dinna ye hear the slogan call?"

Not more quickly sprang that pageant from the silence of the night
Than the army of the people panoplied in freedom's might;
Not more swiftly Concord's message flashed from Boston's Old South spire;
Not more speedily the answer to Clan Alpine's Cross of Fire;
Not more ready Roderick's followers springing at the whistle shrill,
Than the loyal yeoman soldiers starting up from plain and hill.
Not more quickly Highland claymores sank in copse and heathered glen

THE CANDLE PARADE.

Than the grand old army veterans back into the land again.

"One from many," reads our motto, wider, deeper than before—
Not of states but individuals—"We, the people," evermore!
Tell me not of servile soldiers who for king or sovereign died,
Here a million kings and sovereigns marched to victory side by side;
Brothers all in sacred compact, file and captain equal born;
Comrade answering to comrade, waiting for the promised morn.
Far and wide each gleaming taper, "like a good deed," shines abroad,
Till the flaming heights of freedom manifest the will of God.

THE CANDLE PARADE.

But the hill-side's fading beauty tells us the parade is o'er,
Like the embers of the camp-fire dying out forevermore.
Only now in distant windows gleams the candle through the night,
And the camp-fires change to firesides, with their cheery visions bright
Streaming out into the darkness past the lane and wicket-gate,
Where the mother, wife, and sister, all the loved and loving, wait.
Glorious land to live or die for! Let Columbia bend her knee
As she grants her proudest honors to the soldiers of the free.

THE SILENT SOLDIER.

At Mount MacGregor.

[When Grant was dying, a ray of sunlight through the half-closed shutters of his room fell upon Lincoln's picture, leaving the General's portrait, which hung beside it, in deep shadow. After lingering for a moment upon the brow of the martyred President, it passed, at the instant of death, and played upon the portrait of the great General.]

From gulf to lake, from sea to sea,
    The land is draped—a nation weeps;
And o'er the bier bows reverently,
    Whereon the silent soldier sleeps.

The hill-top silhouetted in light
    Salutes the east with outlook wide—
Its name shall live in memory bright—
    The Mount MacGregor, where he died.

THE SILENT SOLDIER.

A monument to stand for aye,
  In summer's bloom, in winter's snows;
A shrine where men shall come to pray,
  While at its base the Hudson flows.

A humble room, the light burns low;
  The morning breaks on distant hill;
The failing pulse is beating slow;
  The group is motionless and still.

Two portraits hang upon the wall,
  Two kindred pictures side by side—
Statesman and soldier, loved by all—
  Lincoln and Grant, Columbia's pride.

A single ray through lattice streams,
  And breaks in rainbow colors there;
On Lincoln's brow a glory gleams
  As wife and children kneel in prayer.

THE SILENT SOLDIER.

A halo round the martyr's head,
    It lights the sad and solemn room;
Above the living and the dead
    The soldier's portrait hangs in gloom—

In shadow one, and one in light:
    But look! the pencil-ray has passed,
And on the hero's picture bright
    The golden sunlight rests at last.

And so, throughout the coming years,
    On both the morning beam shall play,
When the long night of bitter tears
    Has melted in the light away.

www.ingramcontent.com/pod-product-compliance
Lightning Source LLC
Chambersburg PA
CBHW032238080426
42735CB00008B/915